Penguin Modern European P[...]

Advisory Editor: A. Alvarez

Selected Poems · T. Carr[...]

T. Carmi was born in New Y[...]
Hebrew-speaking family, and settled in Israel in 1947, serving
with the Israel Defence Forces for two years and then attending
the Hebrew University. He was Ziskind Visiting Professor of
Humanities at Brandeis University in 1970 and Visiting Fellow of
the Oxford Centre for Postgraduate Hebrew Studies (1974–6).
He has lectured and given poetry readings at many universities
and at the Poetry Center, New York. He took part in the
International Poetry Festival in London in 1971 and in the Poetry
International, Rotterdam in 1975. He has published eight volumes
of poetry in Hebrew, and two collections have appeared in
English translation: *The Brass Serpent* (1964) and *Somebody Like
You* (1971). He has also translated several well-known plays into
Hebrew, including *A Midsummer Night's Dream*. He is preparing an
anthology, *The Penguin Book of Hebrew Verse*.

Dan Pagis was born in Bukowina in 1930 and during the Second
World War was in a concentration camp. In 1946 he went to
Israel where he learnt Hebrew and taught in primary and
secondary schools in a kibbutz and later in Jerusalem, where he
settled in 1956. He had a Ph.D. from the Hebrew University in
Jerusalem and teaches medieval Hebrew literature. In 1968 and
in 1975 he was Visiting Professor at the University of California
U.S.A. He has been publishing poetry in Hebrew since 1946,
translations, mainly from German, and scholarly studies.
His poetry books include *The Shadow Dial* (1959), *Late Leisure*
(1964), *Transformation* (1970) and *Brain* (1975). His scholarly work,
which is quite separate from his poetry, includes books and
articles about Hebrew literature and literary theory in Spain
and Italy during the Middle Ages and the Renaissance. He is
married and has two children.

Selected Poems

T. Carmi   Dan Pagis

Translated by Stephen Mitchell
With an Introduction by M. L. Rosentha

 Penguin Books

Penguin Books Ltd,
Harmondsworth, Middlesex, England
Penguin Books Inc.
7110 Ambassador Road, Baltimore, Maryland 21207, U.S.A.
Penguin Books Australia Ltd,
Ringwood, Victoria, Australia
Penguin Books Canada Ltd,
41 Steelcase Road West, Markham, Ontario, Canada
Penguin Books (N.Z.) Ltd,
182–190 Wairau Road, Auckland 10, New Zealand.

This collection first published 1976
Introduction copyright © M. L. Rosenthal, 1976
Translation copyright © Stephen Mitchell, 1976
The poems by T. Carmi copyright © T. Carmi, 1958, 1961, 1967, 1970, 1974.
Translations of 'Arrow', 'Act One', 'An Apology from the Mirror Man', 'The
Snow God of Abu Tor' copyright © Stephen Mitchell, 1974; translations of
'Quatrains', 'Awakening', 'Listen' copyright © Stephen Mitchell, 1976;
translations of the remaining poems, first published by André Deutsch Limited,
1971, copyright © Stephen Mitchell, 1971
The poems by Dan Pagis copyright © Dan Pagis, 1972, 1974. Translation of
'Brain' copyright © Stephen Mitchell, 1974; translations of the remaining poems,
first published by Carcanet Press, 1972, copyright © Stephen Mitchell, 1972
A number of the translations in this volume have appeared in the *Humanist*,
Present Tense, *Ariel*, *Books*, *P.E.N. Israel 74* and the Introduction in the *Nation*.

Made and printed in Great Britain by
Cox & Wyman Ltd, London, Reading and Fakenham
Set in Monotype Bembo

Contents

Introduction

An outsider coming to Israeli poetry for the first time will inevitably be tempted to see the obvious. He is going to see, more clearly and crudely than an Israeli reader could do, the pressure of Jewish history and culture – the centuries in the Diaspora, the drama of the return, the horror of the holocaust, the Biblical resonance – on whatever he reads. It is a little like the foreigner's overriding consciousness, in reading Baudelaire, that this is an expression of *France*: something a Frenchman would naturally discount in weighing Baudelaire's or any other French poet's quality. But the discounting would be superficial only, a matter of balancing the whole experience. Ultimately, the historical, cultural, national relevance reveals itself sensitively only to intimates of a country's life and language. It reveals itself in a leap from the poem's fingertips to the nerve-ends of such readers. It is not to be coded through a list of motifs and topics, such as may exist in a piece of writing that is itself dead and therefore uncommunicative.

We come to the poems of Dan Pagis and T. Carmi, in the present collection, through the translations of Stephen Mitchell. Mr Mitchell's problem has been enormous; no English version can show us the combinations of harshness and sweetness, and of tradition-deep allusiveness and abrupt colloquial immediacy, of the Hebrew originals. One small instance may suggest the character of the challenge to the translator. In line 6 of Carmi's 'To the Pomegranate Tree', a whole complex of association is involved with one simple visual effect because of the *sound* within which the effect is imbedded. The translator cannot begin to imply the connotations of the repeated Hebrew word *adóm* when it is rendered, properly, into the English *red*.

9

Go away. Go.
Go to other eyes.
I wrote about you yesterday.

I said green
to your branches bowing in the wind,
and red – red – red –
to your fruit shining like dew.
I called light to your dank
obstinate root.

Now you don't exist.
Now you're blocking the day
and the moon that has not yet risen.

Come, beloved
(I wrote about you two days ago,
and your young memory
stings my hands like nettle),
come look at the strange pomegranate tree:
its blood is in my veins, on my head, on my hands,
and it still is planted in its place!

'In line 6,' writes Harold Schimmel, 'the threefold repetition *adóm adóm adóm* ('red red red') echoes the praise of the seraphim in the heavenly spheres: *kadósh, kadósh, kadósh* ('Holy, holy, holy is the Lord of Hosts') of the Hebrew prayerbook.'* While the translator can often weave compensatory effects into the poem, we must nevertheless reconcile ourselves to the loss of such essential values as Mr Schimmel describes. The Mitchell translation of 'To the Pomegranate Tree' does sustain Carmi's atmosphere of inspired though resistant celebration. It was impossible, though, to catch alive that splendid note that re-enacts, in a

* In Stanley Burnshaw, T. Carmi, and Ezra Spicehandler, eds., *The Modern Hebrew Poem Itself* (N.Y.: Holt, Rinehart & Winston, 1965), p. 169.

single line, Carmi's conversion of ritual adoration into a secular, aesthetic exaltation.

Still, translation is not the hopeless affair it seems in our saner moments. Look again at Mitchell's version. He has given us, after all, a window onto Carmi's poem, not only its incantatory imperiousness and wonder but its helpless quarrel with an overmastering symbol. The speaker had at first thought the pomegranate tree merely a source of vivid impressions. Now he sees it possessing his whole being. A striking turn of thought shows him summoning his new love to bear witness to this change. She too has begun to enter his existence in the same way as the tree. The erotic is thus, casually but powerfully, brought into the process the poem describes. Carmi's preoccupation is with the way passionately regarded external reality invades his own very nature. Like an Israeli Lawrence, he has his pomegranate personify a world of fierce knowledge, blood-drenched, sexual and intractable.

Read one way, the poem is clearly touched with the tragic awareness of modern Israel – its possession by a landscape and a history which it wished merely to use for its own creative purpose – but only if we do not labour the point. With most of Carmi's work, indeed, we do better to wait for him to spell out this side of things, in his own usually subtle way. Poems like 'Memorial Day, 1969' and 'A View of Jerusalem' speak explicitly and elegiacally of Israel's griefs and terrors, but such poems make up only a small fraction of his writing. Dan Pagis, on the other hand, is centrally engaged with those griefs and terrors and with a prophetic vision related to them. His full strength is realized in his somewhat Yeatsian poem of coming universal catastrophe, 'The Beginning':

In the ice-filled chaos before the end of creation,
distant fleets of steel are waiting.
Boundaries, in secret, mark themselves.
High above the smoke and the odour of fat and skins hovers

a yellow magnetic stain.
Oblique rays at the pole, alert, quick-eyed,
search for the signal. The code is cracked.
Now that all is prepared for darkness,
a wind, with savage fur, from the horizon, blows
in the hollow bones of mountains,
and at the zero-hour
the Great Bear, blazing, strides forth
in heat. The heavens stand now,
and the earth, and all their hosts.
A time of war.

Despite the grandeur of this vision, its terror is of almost pathological proportions. Chaos resolves itself in a violence all the more frightful because it makes murderous technology a function of the life-principle reduced to mere savagery. 'The odour of fat and skins' that recalls the German concentration camps becomes but a detail in the universal readiness for the coming 'end of creation'.

Pagis lives with the memory of annihilation as something he has both experienced and, of course, been spared. In early adolescence he was a prisoner in a concentration camp in the Ukraine; he escaped in 1944. The past will not hold still in his poems, which cannot help assuming it must return. His work is coloured, too, by guilt at having survived. This guilt is expressed, not through self-castigation, but through a rueful sense of unearned reprieve, neither undesired nor completely welcomed either:

Ready for parting, as if my back were turned,
I see my dead come toward me, transparent and breathing.
I do not accept:
one walk around the square, one rain,
and I am another, with imperfect rims, like clouds.
Grey in the passing town, passing and glad,
among transitory streetlamps,
wearing my strangeness like a coat, I am free to stand ...

('*Ready for Parting*')

Pagis is a poet of survival. He is comparable to Zbigniew Herbert and other Eastern European poets who write out of memories of the concentration camps and the Resistance. But he does not resort to their anti-rhetoric, their almost deadpan restraint. Pagis and other Israeli poets have certainly been affected by the reaction against overt emotionalism in the wake of violence to the human spirit that no verbal violence could match. It is as clear to them as to anyone else that the unspeakable cannot be spoken even though the unbearable has to be borne, and they too have often mastered an astringent and ironic style. They have not, however, had the paralysing political experience, leading to spiritual isolation, of moving from one kind of brutal repression directly into another. An ultimately humanistic and even romantic affirmation is implicit in Israeli thought and life. As Pagis's 'The Beginning' has shown us, this affirmation is anything but a sentimentally optimistic one. It is tragic in character, an affirmation of human meanings however disastrous the human predicament.

'The Beginning' is a total expression of Pagis's tragic and prophetic vision. But he does not devote himself exclusively to the apocalyptic, and I would not wish to discount his simple humanity. We can see it in a quietly compassionate and plainspoken poem such as 'Moments of Old Age' and in the mocking tenderness of 'Europe, Late' – a repossession of that moment when too many people still ignored what was upon them and clung to the illusion that 'everything will be all right'. Pagis unites his prophetic and his colloquial voices in the remarkable poem called 'Written in Pencil in the Sealed Railway-Car'. The title itself would seem to make anything that follows in the poem anticlimactic. It isn't:

> here in this carload
> i am eve
> with abel my son
> if you see my other son

Despite one's first impression, the poem's actual power soon shows itself. Partly this is a matter of the sepulchral force of the Hebrew, the sonorous authority of the primal Biblical names. Partly it is the projected realization of the unspeakable. Sacred text and secular understanding both prove inarticulate before the literal situation commemorated in the title. Eve's thought cannot be completed; identity cannot go beyond the naming of names. The tension between title and poem is between two determinants of Jewish and, by extension, all human consciousness. The poem calls up the implications of an ancient myth whose full meaning, and inadequacy to account for our condition, could not be grasped until our own day.

To write something as crucially relevant and at the same time as brilliantly compressed as this poem may be a matter of inspired luck. The result is almost non-verbal, a breathing archetype. Pagis has projected names and phrases as pigments of bitter consciousness. Or, to change the metaphor, they are acts of invocation that conjure up archaic guilt echoing undiminished into our own moment. He gives us no other poem as directly physical in its utterance as this one in which immediacy and traditional resonance ring out as a single clang of feeling. But three of his short poems ('The Roll Call', 'Testimony', and 'Instructions for Crossing the Border' – separate poems with a shared frame of reference) and one longer poem ('Footprints') have a different and more characteristic sort of success. Literal data of the holocaust appear in these poems too, but their stress is on the begrudging acceptance of survival by one whose real destiny, as it were, was to have been killed as one of the six million. A sense of unreality, almost yet not quite fantasy, is inseparable from being oneself. The thinking in these poems is necessarily metaphorical and paradoxical, and so the poet's idiosyncratic personality and imagination are brought fully into play.

The three shorter poems present the survivor as an 'imaginary man', one who does not appear at the 'roll call' in heaven and who is therefore a 'mistake'. He should be deleted from the records, his eyes 'turned off', his shadow 'erased'. At best, he was made by a 'different creator' from the others and remains curiously unsubstantial:

> And he in his mercy left nothing of me that would die.
> And I fled to him, rose weightless, blue,
> forgiving – I would even say: apologizing –
> smoke to omnipotent smoke
> without image or likeness.

('Testimony')

Rueful at having avoided annihilation, the 'imaginary man' is at once 'not allowed to remember' and 'not allowed to forget'. The long poem 'Footprints' grounds all the paradox and half-fantasy in its literal and personal source, the memory of the time of the 'unloading of the cattle-cars' when the speaker was somehow spared:

> It's true, I was a mistake, I was forgotten
> in the sealed car, my body tied up
> in the sack of life . . .

'Footprints' is a difficult poem. It moves within an ambience of opposed states of existence: escape from death into other-worldly life, and then return once more to the dangerous, death-ridden life of this world. As in the three shorter pieces, Pagis employs an imagery of ambiguous existence in the form of a cloud that moves mysteriously from one state and level of being to another. For instance, the smoke from the bodies cremated in the gas-ovens is an image that blends into the cloud-phase of the speaker's existence. This imagery is intermingled with a birth-imagery sometimes reminiscent of Dylan Thomas's – there are some real affinities between these two poets – with impressions of an imagined realm where seraphim move, and with harshly cruel axe-strokes of realism based on Nazi atrocities. The feeling that this mixture produces is a combined helpless anger, self-directed sarcasm, and visionary buoyancy. The poem moves through recollection of despair and utter moral confusion and *anomie* to a widened view of desolation in the very heavens and then back to something like acceptance of the world's realities without fatuousness or illusion –

> against my will guessing that it's very near,
> inside, imprisoned by hopes, there flickers
> this ball of the earth,
> scarred, covered with footprints.

Too rich for easy summary, the poem proliferates points of reference that sometimes appear as unrelated as the couplets of a *ghazal*. But they do form a complexly unified whole, whose volatile, dynamic, humour-splashed shiftings make this the most rewarding poem by Pagis in the present collection.

Carmi's work hardly ever touches, directly, the nerve of burning historical memory and chagrin that Pagis's does. Indirectly, though, a number of his poems reveal the two poets' reciprocal concerns. Carmi's 'Examination of Conscience Before Going to Sleep' is dedicated, rather pointedly, to Pagis, as though through it Carmi was making a point in a continued friendly debate about the function of poetry. The 'examination of conscience' referred to has no connection, on the surface, with great historical events. It is about a small bird killed by a motor car on the street, passed over by speeding truck drivers and at last kicked into the gutter by a pedestrian. Carmi gives us a sharply drawn vignette of the scene – the people, the sounds, the work going on all around, 'all . . . in broad daylight.' The poem ends:

> I suppose the bird
> is still there, clinging

> to the gutter's edge.
> I note it among the things
> I should forget.

The reverberations of this unpretentious poem are greater than Carmi pretends. It assumes responsibility for what the speaker could hardly have helped, and finds a challenge to conscience in any living being that has been destroyed while oneself has survived. A comparable reverberation arises from Carmi's tiny sequence of two poems called 'Landscapes'. The landscapes are views from a moving train. The first is a charming contemplation of the poetic problem of selecting focal points from among the innumerable apparently trivial details dancing before the eye. The poet makes a necessarily arbitrary decision to use one such detail only, the 'white bird over a green river' with which the poem begins. Yet even this one detail at once splits up into smaller elements, and so the choice must be narrowed even further.

> In fact, I think I'll note
> just one bird.
> Maybe just its wings.

The pathetic bird of 'Examination of Conscience Before Going to Sleep' need not come to mind here, but there *is* a relationship. Carmi's method of structuring his poem engages him with the fundamental aesthetic principle that everything involves everything else, that – as William Carlos Williams's 'The Red Wheelbarrow' has it – 'so much depends' on the implied relationship of sensations and perceptions. He moves from 'a white bird over a green river' to other birds seen in other places, and then to the bushes along the tracks, and then to the whole chaotic mass of things, all the roofs and clouds and blades of grass:

> hard to count from a train,
> so I won't mention them.

But of course he *has* mentioned them. And so, when he returns to the one bird, or at any rate 'just its wings', the whole of life, including the human life that created – and dwells under – the roofs he sees from the train, has been concentered in the one arbitrarily chosen detail of focus.

If it stood alone, the first 'Landscape' would suggest the richness of life rather than its sufferings or our existential guilt at all the pain and death we can do nothing to prevent. The second 'Landscape' alters the case completely. The view glimpsed from the train this time is of a man working with a saw at the top of a tree. Suddenly the passenger sees the man, face contorted with terror and body twisting helplessly, slip and fall. The tone and perspective at the end both parody and deepen the ending of the first 'Landscape'. Though Carmi's literal subject remains far different, these closing lines bring us sharply into the world where Pagis's poetry moves:

> All this I saw
> from the window of a train,
> after a green meadow
> and before a team of horses.
> I note only the fact
> of his falling.
> I didn't hear
> the scream.

Whether or not so intended, this poem 'justifies' Carmi's natural preference for writing a purely lyrical poetry. It suggests what 'Examination of Conscience Before Going to Sleep' states explicitly: the hideous realities that the mind, whatever its state of empathy or level of consciousness, is always to some degree burdened with. In other poems, often, the only sign of such a burden is a melancholy shading of tone as the speaker pursues an elusive notion or feeling – the 'tears from the depth of some divine despair' that are so distinguishing a mark of the lyrical tradition, East or West. One such poem is 'Somebody Like You', about the difficulty of discovering the true mind of a sleeping child. Another is 'No News', about a moment of unexpectedly felt emptiness in the midst of deep and lonely meditation. Carmi's love-poems, too, depend for their intensity of feeling on a sense of loss and guilt as well as on their exploration of the subjective meaning of passion. These poems, especially 'The Sacrifice', 'The Claim', and 'Those Who Go on Voyages', are not self-lacerating in the manner of Lowell or Plath. They plunge, rather, into the actual sense of an infinitely valued personal unfolding within an experience. But each experience has had its cost which must be explored as well, in the same way that the train-ride of 'Landscapes' exacted its emotional expenditure.

Carmi's finely responsive and resilient sensibility stamps his poems with a pervasive anticipation of discovery. They are magnetically engaging. A poem like 'Through the Windows' is an absolutely delightful composition of lights and darks and touches of sound. 'Girl in the Closet' is touching and sympathetic and yet 'heartless' – 'simple and faithless' – in the age-old sense of the poet as objective observer of his own emotional relationships. Carmi has an elegant, intimate disinterestedness that is the obverse side of his capacity for empathy. He is one of those who, in the midst of tragic life and themselves committed to humane loyalties, still insist on savouring whatever life genuinely has to offer.

I have, perhaps, not given enough attention to some parallel qualities of Pagis's. Certainly his poetry does not exist at a lower level of 'purity' – that is, of poetic rigour – than Carmi's, but his expressed concerns are more drastic. He succeeds in making a singing poetry out of the materials of disaster and in getting beyond the clichés of politics and of a Spenglerian portentousness to which he might be prone. When he turns away from historical and prophetic concerns, the tone is usually still drastic. Often, as in 'Snake' and 'Already' and many other poems, he has the same doom-driven dismay that we find in Dylan Thomas. He, too, is obsessed with the knowledge that death rides hard on the heels of birth, and that we are hurried irresistibly through the process by the force that through the green fuse drives the flower. Carmi's dead bird in the gutter and his man falling from the tree are equally victims of this pressing force of natural change, but Pagis is far more taken up with the indignity of our condition, the fact that we are quick-marched through life's changes before we can even think to get anything in order. Even when Pagis's poems are abstractly metaphysical in character, as in 'Final Examination' or in the beautiful 'Twelve Faces of the Emerald', in which he comes closer than anywhere else to a purely image-centred technique, they remain chained to reality by an armed and uncompromising sensibility. But sometimes, just sometimes, as in 'Come' or in 'Seashell', he shows himself a mystic of the same sensed awareness as I have attributed to Carmi. An urgent desire – a lust – to isolate spiritual resources that will make us as strong as possible in the face of history's savage blows while we remain responsively open to reality and the creative possibilities within it may be endemic to the modern mind. If so, these two Israeli poets are compellingly accurate spokesmen for that mind, as well as for their own country's special and precarious poise and for their own very individual natures.

T. Carmi

Arrow

Against its will drawn back
and shot.
It cleaves the air
talking in the language
of hawk and gull.
At half way
it still remembers
the bow,
the hand that strung it.
From there it belongs
to nothing but its end:
the round heart
where it will stick
quivering.

The Unicorn Looks in the Mirror

Madam,
had you not held this mirror
to my face,

I would never have known
that I am melancholy, that my neck
is proud, that only one horn
grows from my forehead, and my beard
is wispy, and my lips too thick.

Madam,
let there be no anger,
no reproach – for had your bitter hand
not held this mirror
to my face,

I would never have dared
to approach, to rest
my cloven hooves
on your lap.

Madam,
had you not summoned my body's
echo, we would never
have become three:
I, and you, and my self,
and above us
a horn,
lengthening.

The Stranger

Opposite the painting
the stranger passes his finger
over the frame, and his eyes
bite into the indifferent apple.

The stranger, on the banks of the rug,
stops, extends
a hesitating foot. He sits down
slowly, and the chair
asks him many questions
behind his back.
Afterwards, he looks through the window
and recognizes a bare tree,
waiting in the cold, on a mountain ridge,
and one bird.

*

The trouble is,
he must hurry from place to place.
The trouble is, on the next day
he will see tooth-marks in the flesh of the apple,
the rug rising to greet him, the armchair
rubbing against his leg like a cat.
The stranger needs to uproot himself from here,
tomorrow, in order to plant
another bird in his eyes.

*

Will you come to me today, tonight?
And if you come – who are you?

But, at this moment,
as I stand opposite the window-frame,
I have the right to ask.

Landscapes

I

A white bird over a green river; two;
then three.
One telegraph-pole; two;
three bushes.
More than that (roofs,
clouds, blades of grass)
is hard to count from a train,
so I won't mention them.
In fact, I think I'll note
just one bird.
Maybe just its wings.

2

He was standing at the top of a tree,
dressed in blue overalls,
sawing.

      Suddenly
his face gaped,
his body twisted like a branch,
his hands filled with wind,
and he fell.

All this I saw
from the window of a train,
after a green meadow
and before a team of horses.
I note only the fact
of his falling.
I didn't hear
the scream.

Song of Friendship

My friend, my brother, dearest of all my friends,
For whom I would walk through fire and the many waters.
And one day I felt the army of his eyes
On the back of my neck; he said: 'I wish you were

Dead.' Oh angels scurried up and down;
A cow – naked! – hiccuped on the roof;
Pomegranates split like thunder; vines
Shed their skins; an ocean froze like ashes.

My friend, my brother, understood my mind;
To him the chambers of my heart were opened
Wide; he came, went, planted dreams in me;
He asked, solved; committed me to death.

Since then I'm very careful: in the kitchen,
In the pool, and at major intersections.

Songs without a Name

When you give a child the name of a bird —
it loses the bird.
JOYCE CARY

I'm only saying these things,
because they began and ended a long time ago;
if I didn't know what their end was,
I would be able to write them as poems.

1

All night I couldn't sleep: I was biting your name in the pillow, and your name wept till dawn. All night the hangers in the closet made music, like triangles in a children's orchestra.

2

I'm choking you with my body. Only one thing can justify this abomination: that you are the air I breathe.

3

My hands are quiet like the window of your room, filled with clouds and air: my eyes are opened wide: the thing, and not its opposite.

4

It was only yesterday that you told me your name, and already it is swarming within me like schoolboys at recess. Only yesterday – and already it is swooping within me, like gulls toward the floating bread.

5

All these people in the streets, all these masks – do they love? I must put on a mask. Otherwise my face will be lost in the yards and in the rivers.

6

A clear mirror before your face and your hand. I put my hand on your breast. I put my mother beside you. And my childhood rises within me, and falls asleep.

7

Your sleep builds no wall or city of refuge. You let me walk around in the shadow of your eyelashes. My head on your shoulder, and your palm open.

8

They laugh at us, and they're right. The lamp burns without candles, the floor flows without shores, the window is always open. We have forgotten what it means to close. We remember everything; we laugh, and we're right.

I'm only saying these things,
because they began and ended a long time ago;
if I hadn't seen what their end was,
I would have written them as poems.

9

I can still explain to all of you what a lie is. Like someone who has been there on a visit, for a short time, many years ago.

10

My thirty-five years. I will open them one by one, put you in each one of them like cinnamon into an antique spice-box. When the day comes, they will all understand that I carried your fragrance inside me. Against their will they will answer, Amen.

11

I walk in the street, spring within spring, and think the thoughts of the coming winter. My eyes are veiled with snow, my hands still warm.

29

12

The night-birds that you put inside me fly away at dawn.
But I know that wherever I shut my eyes they will return.
Like your hand to my head.

13

Our beginning still laughs; therefore let us count the ends:
once I saw a sudden bird hit a windowpane and break its
neck; once I watched a premature spring abandon its fruit to
the frost; once, on my flowing bed, drought gushed within
me.

14

On the birthday of her love, she dressed in black. From her
feet to her festive hair, her clothing was black. His hand
became bony, his eyes flamed. He understood, he touched
her, and all her black answered:

15

Not after my death, and not in twenty years, and not in a
week. Tomorrow – what will remain tomorrow? Oh, we are
changing into ancient things. Time flows over us, the clouds
polish our faces. We are being gathered.

I'm only saying these things,
because even then we began
to collect each other.

16

Your name tears open my eyes in the morning, and shuts
    them at night.
I do not say much.
You know.
Your name shuts my eyes to the morning, and tears them
    open to night.

17

This wind will stop and this flower will fade. This house will collapse and this man will fall. This woman will sin and my sin will die with her. We will remain, with words that blossom for one night, that have no cycle, no season, no bed.

18

I wrap myself in you each morning. My lips move, my legs are dumb. There is no point in asking when I do not give. There is no point in begging when you do not refuse. There is no point in singing.

I'm only saying these things.
You cannot bless the new moon
when you stand still.

19

The street was empty. Strange children came and wrote your name. I erased everyone with a giant sponge.

20

The moment I pause, you begin to move toward me. The moment I stop in my flight, you blow at me from all sides. I mustn't linger.

21

My memory kneels and tenses like a runner. When the signal is given, I am wrenched from your night and from you. My heart drums. My lungs scream toward the finish-line.

22

Your name gets smaller and smaller in my terrified skies. I am transporting you to a land that has no borders, passports, customs-officers. I have no belongings to hide, nothing to declare. But that field – it is entirely mine. A heritage forever and oblivion.

23

Yes, I'm always ready to run away. All I need is a crevice, a slit like the pupil of a skinny cat's eye. If you shut your eyes for an instant, the darkness will be my door. And when I return, I will touch the doorposts of your face, and my hand will not come back clean.

24

In order to clean the windowpane, you must soil it.
In order to return, you must turn.
I turn to you and ask:
Where should I go now that the answer has been given
and I can no longer return?

25

Your name gets smaller and smaller. The air grows empty.
Already I cannot divide firmament from firmament.

I have only said these things,
because I knew what their end was.
Now I am ready again,
and wait for the sound of the wings of a large bird
that doesn't know a thing:
not the name of a season,
not the address of a nest,
not the direction of a wind.
I am waiting for the sound of the wings of a large bird
that doesn't know my name.

Those Who Go on Voyages

Those who go on voyages seldom come back holy.
THOMAS À KEMPIS

1

Even before he set forth
he already had the face of a man
who must double back:

unshaven, one of his eyes
servile, the other one dodging
the camera's quick trap.

He filled out the forms in a hurry,
he was all ready to go,
had a date with a strange tongue:

cracked mounds in the garden,
a woman growing wild,
cobwebs of old words in the nursery.

Then he said to his friends:

O my friends, o my dear ones,
water and fix, spray and prune –
I'll be back soon.

2

Then he set forth:

He clambered up the ladder
which her high dream had placed,
he skipped up and called to her: follow me! –

and brandished his foot above her.

He descended and ascended and descended,
he bumped and he shoved and he thumped
all the angels he met.

Then he stopped on the way:

All at once he opened his years
like an antique spice-box,
and filled them with the strange fragrance.

Oh myrrh and mountains of frankincense,
we have a little sister; this
is the day, and what shall we do?!

We'll talk. And he went on his way.

He flew toward the naked light:
barren, barren – he cursed –
who bore me in wrath, still-born.

He slammed his eyes and said:
my love hasn't gone to eternity,
only to the next room.

Then he lingered on the way:

He sat in the street, pleading:
I have no defenses at all,
like a snail out of its shell;

entered the strange house,
flooded it with brightness,
then left – and forgot to switch it off.

He nested in the street, chirping:
O my soul – o cover my cage
with a black curtain, and I'll be quiet;

rested his head on her breast,
rested his head like a stone,
then left – and forgot to roll it off.

I'm only a broken statue:
the soles of my feet are waiting
for the wisdom of expert hands;

gave her his prowess as a present,
the smile of his youth as a tip,
then left – and forgot to leave it.

Then he set forth:

Near ones, good-bye, dear ones,
forget me not, sweetie, the photographer's
waiting for the other eye.

He opened both eyes and surrendered them:
drooled onto his image
and thirstily drank his face.

Then he set forth:

He declared everything, candidly:
so many dead angels
(the gift of my clumsy foot),

and a ladder (not mine) for sale;
so many bags of second-hand
sand from holy places.

And then? Then he came back.

3
She was waiting for him at the dock,
to receive him, face to face.

Her hair – old cobwebs;
the child trapped in her palm.

Her flesh was like a sieve,
she was dressed in lace:

the nights had eaten her alive.
He cried, he wailed;

his tears fell
onto her live wounds.

She cried, of course she cried.
Then they set forth.

4
Those who go on voyages
seldom come back holy.

He wasn't holy when he left.
No wonder he came back.

Still Life

As they sat together, silent
in the blazing sun,
a full moon came and blessed them.

Her fingers dripped love,
his eyes shut in wax.

These lovers!

How they brought upon us
a night exceedingly white
in the noon of day.

Quatrains

Love Me, Love My Dog

Sin crouches at the door — GENESIS 4:7

He no longer crouches at the door
like a well-trained dog. It's cold outside.
Now he's curled up by the fire,
and his master guards him, carefully.

Attention

It's hard for two conches to have a serious talk.
Each one pays attention to its own sea.
Only a pearl-diver or an antique-dealer
can state without hesitation: the same sea.

Boardwalk

Small breasts like seashells.
If I put my ear to them,
I will hear the beautiful night-fishes moving
sinuously in my depths.

Girl in the Closet

What does my coat tell you
when you shut yourself, barefoot, in the closet?
And my big shoes –
two wells of evil shadows?
What do my empty pockets tell you,
and my pants, wrapped around your neck?

I can only guess.
Your muted crying leads an orchestra
of hangers and hooks.
Your face follows the darkness
like a sick sunflower.

I stand in the lighted room and say nothing.
You will have to get out
by your own tears, by your own hands:
the key is in my empty pocket.

No News

There is no one tonight in the courtyards of the moon.
Except for the winter mulberry-branches
and my clinging eyes –
there is no one.

There is no one tonight in the courtyards of the moon.
Except for the mulberry-tangles
and your consuming memory –
there is no one.

Is there a spell for this hour?
Except for the women spinning
and my streaming blood –
there is no sound.

There is no one tonight in the courtyards of the moon.

Awakening

Come, put your hand upon my mouth.
I'm not used to this light.

Our love is bat-like: flies
darkly in jagged circles: does not miss.
Your face explains to me
my hands. What will I understand
in the light?
Come, put your hand upon me.

My sleep (what time is it?)
hugged your childhood. Ten
between sea and night, midnight between
me and you, seven
between the lattices of dawn.
Oh no, I'm not used to this light

which comes to open my eyes
like cold pinholes. In the scale
of the gunsight I will weigh
my blindness and the fear
of your dust. Come,
put your hand inside me.

Face to face, will I still have
one? I might be quiet,
or talk.
Come, put your hand upon my mouth.
I'm not used to this light.

Listen

Listen to the empty house
whistling in the storm!
Still unfloored, unwalled,
unpainted –
listen to it singing
with all its strings!
I've never heard a finished house
trumpeting this way in the autumn wind.

Last Confession

Eye to eye.
The white moon grinds my light
like millstones.

Forehead to forehead.
The full moon swells on my flesh
like leeches.

Mouth to mouth.
The holy moon swallows my air
like locusts.

Beloved,
for you I dance,
to you my nights are vowed.

I have no other shroud.

The Claim

I

No letters, photographs, dedications.
Now we are in the hands of memory.

I'm glad you didn't give me this autumn,
the moment when sea gives in to moon.

No scratches, love-wounds, bites.
Our flesh says only first rain.

I'm glad I didn't give you that night,
the moment of the muezzin.

On the day of judgement – they will all, all, rush to the bench.
And we will stand there, innocent, without fear.

2 THE WITNESSES

Two sunsets (autumn) on the shores of the Mediterranean,
a pair of horses who came to plunder the evening sands,
a salt wind that watched our tongues,
a fat woman sizzling like a frying-pan, in a deserted café,
chairs stacked up behind us like dossiers –

'They darkened the eyes of the earth
unsheathed a branch from its leaves
destroyed our dream like locusts
blotted out yes they blotted out earth's memory –'

Twilights, two, on the hills of Jerusalem,
children, hidden in the bushes, who threw stones at us,
eternal soldiers (ours) painted on the wall of an emplacement,
a coat of arms hanging on the gate of a hotel,
a lock tensed like a listening ear –

'They didn't talk
they opened the floodgates of silence
brought an end to our flesh
rose yes they rose very high –'

We are ready for the verdict. All the truth, hand and thigh.
But the trial, in fact, is superfluous:
lovers are always guilty from the first
to the last of their limbs.

3 WHO BY FIRE

Fire is a natural symbol of life and passion, though it is the one
element in which nothing can actually live
SUSANNE K. LANGER

Your honour:
always with torches, with fire familiar and strange,
with parades, with rocketing words,
moaning of sirens, heroics,
desperate ladders to heaven –

always with torches, with masks of the salamander,
echoes of I-am, flare of the phoenix,
split-tongued seraphim,
sparks and voices from heaven –

always with torches, with rain-haloed moons,
tides that smoulder and fan,
broken-lunged runners,
billowing, receding horizons –

Your honour:
always with torches, and at dawn, ash.
But perhaps this once
                    (we confess, have confessed our guilt)
air, and earth, and water.

4

We came down upon the ridge like spring rain.
The surprised colours cried out and the smells burst
    from all sides.
No, we didn't mean to awaken. But the painted soldiers
    on the sides of the emplacement
woke up – we stood without cover – fired!
A volley of old eyes –
then they sank back into ambush.
So many years in the rain and wind and oblivion.
No, we didn't mean to stir up. But eyes, an army of eyes,
    bloomed in her hand.
They passed over me in single file. They examined
    all the lines of my hands, asked my back
if it would turn, my face – would it fall.
Eyes, an army of laughing eyes, shut upon me without fear.
The sun set innocently, the children rose.
They threw sad stones at us,
    and shouted in a strange tongue.
We got up and left. No stone hit us.
No stone could hit us.

5   WHO BY THE SWORD

A sword is above us on Jerusalem's hills
sharp upon our necks
                        and we are double-edged

A sword is above us in the target's grove
drawing out our eyes
                        and we are double-edged

The thrust of the distance and the border's howl
a siege of birds and a treetop's flash

A sword is above us on Jerusalem's hills
biting and raging
                        swallowing our air

But we will stand there naked
(Oh little spies, eyes upside-down!)

We will stand there without breathing
A sword is above us on Jerusalem's hills

But again we will turn over
                              mouth-to-mouth

6 WHO BY WATER
Your honour:
it was the sea, the sea.
I couldn't comb my hair.
Do not look down upon me because my head is disheveled.

We sat on the beach,
there was a strong wind.

Sir:
it was the sea, the sea.
I can hardly hear.
Please speak up.

We sat on the sand, in the wind,
close together,
and were filled with the whisper of hands,
the thunder of sea-shells.

Your honour:
it was the sea, the sea.
I can't see you.
Do not look down upon me because I'm invisible.

We sat on the beach,
there was a strong wind.
The sea answered, we didn't ask.
The fishermen reeled in their rods.
The sun set.

High priests blessed us.
I was afraid to look her in the face.

7 HER DREAM

I am sailing in a ship of windows.
My eye is glued to the side –
            a dappled gold-fish.
The ship sails on.
A cloud of my breath hides
his house from my eye.
I cannot say a thing.

1964

Act One

I've been waiting for you since morning.
You appear, single,
like any person at all.
I notice the colour of your coat.
That blue, I know
It will come back at me some day.
Your head reaches my shoulders.
It was always like this; your mark,
pale as chalk, still
on my collar-bone.

Suddenly, as I touch your neck,
you turn into a thousand women.
My chameleon memory
shuts its crossed eyes
and drops, spent, naked.
Your hair closes on me
in waterfalls of silence and night,
a thousand hands, a million eyelashes –
and you pour into me, through me.

I stand like a beggar in the doorway,
cursing my paltry limbs,
in despair of my ten fingers,
loathing my narrow forehead,
my thin lips,
praying to the sand on the shore.

From beneath the table a train charges out
whistling.

The abandoned station rises like mist.
Gulls circle in the kitchen
and the bedroom flows out to the quai.
Kindly old men
smile at us from the nursery.

My God, cries my body,
whither shall I flee from your faces,
from their faces.
And I:
one moment fire, one moment wind,
one moment man, one moment woman,
and water, water,
one moment gasps, one moment gills –
where shall I go without a name?

Enter the messenger
(gas, milk, electricity),
his eyes ticking like clocks.
In a wild fright thousands of you
rush back into your body,
hide in the blue depths of your coat.
I hear, with some relief,
the last gull banging its way
out the kitchen door.

For the time being,
since we're just flesh, just blood,
we've come to the end.
You are leaving me,
as you appeared, single,
like any person at all.

Transition

The eucalyptus shattered the autumn nights.

Oh what a shameless lament!
In the moon's eye
it cracked the silence of windows,
plucked sleep from the birds.
What an abomination
thus to scatter among us
all the shreds of its days!

And now
(what a wailing there was!)
now it stands
on the mound of its silent skins,
ruddy and soft,
in the heart of another season.

Four Air-Letters

1

I burned your letter.
It's autumn now.
Tatters of bark hang
from the eucalyptus trunk,
like clothes that are out of style.
I piled up its leaves; it flamed,
changed to ashes.
Then I took off my shoes, sat
for seven days and seven nights,
waiting for the little phoenix
to rustle its wings.

Oh I shall brood over these ashes
until my soul takes flight.

2

A scrap of shoulder,
part of an ear,
an eye like a grape.
All have joined in a sudden
plot to deceive me.
I go on putting you together
like a jigsaw puzzle.
I go on calculating
you and the end of days.

Soon you will be held in my hands,
redeemed,
whole.

3
Now the clocks are changing:
your time is carried on the waves,
skips like a dolphin.
Mine trudges upon heavy earth.

What happens to sundials at night?
What happens to hourglasses
and angel-wings in water?

But when you tell me,
I'll tell you how many grains
of sand, and how many stars,
and how much the time is.

4
I'm sending you many words today,
equipped with light and air and emergency
oxygen masks.

But they have a long way to go,
and who knows
if they've got enough wind.

When they reach you, my love,
you may have to revive them,
mouth to mouth.

Night of Mirrors

At your side – and my dream is on you,
is in you, and at your side. I enter
and your breath says: 'Come,
she is waiting for you like darkness
for the opened eye. You were here,
now you are doubled, tripled.
She waits for you, all, like light for sunrise.
Like a beach for the echoes of the rain.'

At your side – and my dream is of you,
is in you, and at your side. And your breath.

Aquarelle

Silence around me, as water over the sea
Tiny bright-coloured lives
Our mouth filled with water and song

Now I am the wave that lifts you
Now the soft light, the shadow
And the spear

Carefully, carefully we listen
To the transformations within us
To the code of the moon and the shadow

Of the spear.

To the Pomegranate Tree

Go away. Go.
Go to other eyes.
I wrote about you yesterday.

I said green
to your branches bowing in the wind,
and red – red – red –
to your fruit shining like dew.
I called light to your dank
obstinate root.

Now you don't exist.
Now you're blocking the day
and the moon that has not yet risen.

Come, beloved
(I wrote about you two days ago,
and your young memory
stings my hands like nettle),
come look at the strange pomegranate tree:
its blood is in my veins, on my head, on my hands,
and it still is planted in its place!

Condition

First I'll sing. Afterwards, perhaps I'll talk.
I'll return to the words I said

like a man rehearsing his face at dawn.
I'll retrace my silences

as the moon wanes.
I'll swing the cry-bird around and around my head

like a boy drawing his sword at Purim.
I'll court your closed hands

like a lantern growing endlessly black. Yes,
I'll return, I'll be silent, I'll cry,

and I'll sing. First I'll sing. I'll wrap the words
in paper bags, like pomegranates.

And afterwards, perhaps we'll talk.

Transformation

A moth fell on me this morning.
With a flick of a dark wing it erased
all the correct birds,
the smell of coffee, a crying baby (mine),
and in the distance – a whistling train, the rhythm of
   hammers.

Gradually the morning returns to me:
large, exultant, false.
If anyone's face lights up
at me, I will look
for the shadow of the wing in his eyes.

An Apology from the Mirror Man

The truth is, things are rough.
From too much use in light and also in the dark,
from too much polishing,
in sun, neon, moon,
his edges have rusted,
his face has become dull.
You stand in front of him,
come a little closer, turn sideways, breathe on his eyes:
'Mirror, mirror . . .'
It's not that he doesn't know what to answer.
He knows. Something in him remembers:
a rainbow in a cloud, summer lightning,
quicksilver beneath the corrosion.
But the truth is, he's tired.
He sinks, slowly, into himself,
and turns his other side to you.
Please don't look into his eyes.
He is asking for a little quiet
and forgiveness.

Spectrum

for Moshe Spitzer

1 BLACK

Let us lock the doors
with seven locks and a bolt
let us close the shutters
let us turn off the lights

and let us assume

with a quiet shadowy voice
like someone speaking out of sleep
like water in the heart of a well

let us assume

without mirror
repentance or atonement
once and for all and this one time

let us assume

that these are the last words
which will leave my mouth

2 THE CHAMELEON'S WORDS

My ear was glued to the window-screen
My tongue was inviting flies to dinner

I heard the end that you never spoke
I was shadowy as your darkness

Now I'll redden like a pomegranate
get greener than an almond

I can't help it
There's a rainbow in my blood

Every time I fall
a different colour awakens in me

My dreams are very colourful
I heard the end that you never heard

3   RED
A sea of pomegranates throbs within my eyes
A well of life, a well of life
The moon will dance before me
To bless my nights

A jubilee of sunlight is trumpeting my name
I shall not want, I shall not want
The hours will awaken me
To scarlet praise

The voices of the spring-rain are rising through my days
You're pardoned now, you're pardoned now
For every man is rash, is false
And a sea in his eyes.

Blessing of the Moon

1

The light-years are shut off,
the many waters quenched.

An ancient echo tells me
my blood still flows.

But if I keep on sitting here,
staring,

instantly
I'll turn into a fossil.

2

A child will pick me up,
like a snail,
and say:
Look, you can still see the spirals
of his smile.

A fragile woman, cabbalist of style,
will put me upon her shelf,
among amber beads and a vase
and dewy souvenirs of herself.

She will wait for the oohs and aahs:
So young, and already a fossil!

3

Won't I be able to get up,
to climb out of this well,

to frighten the passers-by
with guesses of moss?

Too late.
Stay where you are.
Your hair has turned white.

Through the Windows

The windows are open,
and light-fish swim secretly into all the rooms.
Now they will nibble at the bait of our eyes,
and the fisherman will calmly laugh.

Flooded by twilight,
we will sink quietly in our rooms,
far from the help of the riverbank
and the fisherman's laughter.

Examination of Conscience Before Going to Sleep

for Dan Pagis

The driver wasn't even aware
that he'd run over the little bird.
Suddenly it had a name
and address, a colour to its wings.
It lay in the middle of the street,
thrown onto its back,
feet lifted in a diagonal V.
Strange,
even truckdrivers noticed it now,
spread over it
a whistling tunnel. Finally
a pedestrian came
and gave it a last kick.

All this happened in broad daylight,
to the sound of buzzsaws
from a nearby carpenter's shop.
Meanwhile night has come.
I suppose the bird
is still there, clinging
to the gutter's edge.
I note it among the things
I should forget.

The Sacrifice

Even though Isaac did not die, Scripture honours him as if he
had died and his ashes had been strewn upon the altar.
MIDRASH HAGADOL

Last night I dreamt that my son did not return.

He came to me and said:
When I was little and you were,
you would not tell me
the story of the binding of Isaac,
to frighten me with knife, fire, and ram.

But now you have heard her voice.
She whispered, didn't even command –
(her hand full of voices and she
said to your forehead, to your eyes:)
is it
so?
And already you ran to the hiding-place,
drew out the knife, fire, and ram
and in a flash
your son, your only one.

Last night I dreamt that my son did not return.
I waited for him to come home from school,
and he was late.
And when I told her,
she put her hand upon me
and I saw all the voices
he had seen.

Somebody Like You

You must hurry in order to hear
what the sleeping child said.

When you arrive
the muted syllables have already sunk
back into his dream.

You must hurry in order to be there
when they lick the shore, come
to rest.

Somebody, somebody like you
must identify them in the light.

In Memory of Leah Goldberg

1

A pigeon and a crow
live on the tiles of my house.
A little boy sees them
and says:
God's playing checkers on the roof.

2

A sudden gust of pigeons.
They felt the hurled air before I did.
Now the windows shriek,
and the boom is in my ears.
Leah is dead.
The pigeons are small in the sky.

3

This patch of sky is hers.
She fenced it in
with a few lines, a few stanzas,
and put a bird there.
The little bird flies on patrol
and chases away all the scarecrows.

4

She used to stand at her window for hours:
outside she saw a horse's tail
flicking away the sirocco,
another window shutting its owner,
another window staring like a lake,
a window with a mezuzah
for guests from another season,
a window where a bee crouches

with hair on its belly.
No, she said,
take this bee away.
I am inside, it is outside.
No, she said.

5

She used to sit at her window for hours,
like a collector with a magnifying glass.

6

She had a boyfriend, three years old,
who gave her his hand as she walked down the garden stairs.
As soon as she touched his hand,
the cement split open
and they disappeared among the waves of roses.

7

She loved Chagall,
and wasn't ashamed of that.
She loved,
and was ashamed.
She could refuse to love,
and wasn't ashamed of that either.

I never saw more
than one flower
in her room.

Shockwaves

The air is hurled, is hurling.
I look at your forehead:
widening swirls, circle
chasing circle, chased, growing
in the expanses of your brow,
between your eyelids of day
and your hair at night.

O my mirror, now all is mixed together:
my face, a piece of sky, wisp of cloud, wing, leaf –
widening banks, swirls
of white stone and night stone.
I'm sorry for your forehead.

Meanwhile there's someone as high as my thigh
and someone as high as my eyes –
learning to look in our mirrors,
to tell the image from its double,
the reflection from its water;
and afterwards they will have to learn
how much one must forget
and how one learns, like us, not to remember,
how not to remember –

But the air is hurling, the air is hurled,
O my mirror, forehead, face –
the soul of you, the body of you!
The soul and the body
are not ours.

Memorial Day, 1969

In Memory of Y. H.

1

She orders vegetables by phone
and arranges, arranges the house.
It's hard to think about her.
There are terrifying screams in her navel
but the line has been disconnected.
It's hard to think about her.
If she is connected –
it's only to the earth:
an ear of flesh and blood to an ear of dust,
and she listens, she listens to the terrifying voices.
It's hard to think about her.

2

He goes to work in the morning,
his chin cries
and his sunglasses laugh.
I met him at noon.
His eulogy was brief:
'It'll be three months tomorrow,
he got an A-minus on his finals.'
I was afraid to look at him as he left:
loaded with dirt and rock,
a porter of memories –
how will he manage to cross the street?
I was afraid to look at his face:
a man without a profile,
without a now –
how can you shake his hand?
He is missing a dimension,
and he doesn't have time.

3

We discussed the margins and the typeface.
I too like precision,
and many dates are written in my notebook.
On other pages are:
a shorthand account of night-birds,
and terrifying voices at noon;
syllables of panic,
and silences, in a first draft.

A View of Jerusalem

To Tamara

1

Soft light, green
of treetops – one green,
the fir; another,
the pine. A blue nest in the middle
for the morning bells – one bell
for the fir; another
for the pine.
    That is what the eyes see,
that is what the ears hear
in the northern window. There is nothing,
nothing like Jerusalem,
in which this distance says
something obscure, muted
and explicit.
    The birds see the sound,
my wife sees the birds,
and I cannot lie to her.
There is nothing.

2

Child, child, little flower,
can I already play with you at words?
If I say to you that mine is ours,
that the button opens and none can close,
that the flower closes and none can open –
                    come here beside me.
Even when the sun is shining,
walk in the middle of the street.
When the street-lamp is before us,
put your shadow in mine.
When the street-lamp is behind us,

your hand in mine.
                         Always be visible,
within range of eye and voice,
and I will teach you games of hide-and-seek.

3
Naked. Bone, stone, sky.
Sirens drain our blood,
air foams in the wake of their sound.
Open wide. Dust – blind – and ashes.
Windowpanes make room for eyes,
eyes for the sound of sirens.
That is all a man is, now.
                              Take off your clothes.
I have to touch you.
Now.

4
Everyone speaks in song:
thinks one thing,
and says another;
says one thing,
and thinks.

A winter landscape filled with clocks.
A man puts on his smile like a coat.
Don't look at the lining.

The mine is a name.
The raid is a door.
The trap is a part.
There is no thing
that does not compel its opposite.

A grammar of fears.
The rules – extremely sudden,
and it's hard to talk.

One thing is clear:
everyone plays.
And another thing:
you are no exception.

5
Now. Tomorrow will surely come,
in my window.
And the walls without a window?
The windows covered with stone?

My wife sees the birds
hidden,
her eyes wide open.
I see my wife:
in the noon of night,
a silver dome at her right hand;
in the dark of day,
at her left a dome of gold.

Sirens in the eyes
and stones from a wall.
(Flash of entangled horns.
A nail glittering in the Roman sun.)
A stone rises
like a small cloud –
                    child, child,
little hand,
can I already say to you Jerusalem,
soft light, tomorrow, another green.

(*after the Mahaneh Yehudah explosion, 1969*)

The Snow God of Abu Tor

His eyes were knives.
His mouth – a red bracelet.
His nose – a carrot, of course.

We worshiped him all day,
we leaped in front of him shamelessly.
And at night, in the light of his pale creature,
we danced before his fulminating eyes,
his lips of carbuncle,
his bright flocks scattered over the earth.

O king of one night,
high and mighty ancient of a day,
O snow god!

We knew that your end is looming.
Before our battered eyes
you are turning to memory.
The bracelet goes back to the closet.
The carrot and the knives to the kitchen.
The child to the classroom.

And we, our mouths dry from praising,
stand in the sun-drenched yard
searching for white footprints.

Dan Pagis

In the Laboratory

The Last Ones

I am already quite scarce. For years
I have appeared only here and there
at the edges of this jungle. My graceless body
is well camouflaged among the reeds and clings
to the damp shadow around it.
Had I been civilized,
I would never have been able to hold out.
I am tired. Only the great fires
still drive me from hiding-place to hiding-place.

And what now? My fame is only in the rumours
that from time to time
and even from hour to hour
I wane.
But it is certain that at this moment
someone is tracking me. Cautiously
I prick all my ears and wait. The steps
already rustle the dead leaves. Very close. Here.
Is this it?

Am I it? I am.
There is no time to explain.

In the Laboratory

The data in the glass beaker: a dozen scorpions
of various species – a swarming, compromising
society of egalitarians. Trampling and trampled upon.
Now the experiment: an inquisitive creator blows
the poison gas inside
and immediately
each one is alone in the world,
raised on its tail, stiff, begging the glass wall
for one more moment.
The sting is already superfluous;
the pincers do not understand;
the straw body waits for the final shudder.
Far away, in the dust, the sinister angels
are afraid.
It's only an experiment. An experiment. Not a judgement
of poison for poison.

The Readiness

I too, like all the apes in the neighbourhood,
grumble from branch to branch:
the past age, which was filled with sun, has passed.
Now it's cold. The nuts are too hard.
The carnivores are getting more and more supple.

This is it, I'm emigrating. Good-bye.

Hey, what's happening,
my tongue's tied in knots,
my shoulders, where are my shoulders,
suddenly I've got stature,
erectness,
suddenly I'm threatened with
what, a high brow!
Bulbs, flickering bulbs!

How good this silence is. Gradually
I pick out an attractive suit,
get dressed,
light up a cigarette,
and sit down with the stop-watch, my only friend,
beside the table, in perfect readiness
for the invention of chess.

The Cave Man Is Not About to Talk

At time's tail-end my great-grandchildren's great-
Grandchildren pause,
My skull in hand, and try to calculate
The centuries I ground between my jaws.

And what news of the mammoth will they wrest
From my laconic mouth? I've got time:
I'm not about to talk. They haven't guessed
My profile, even. Fine,

Let them enjoy the bones that I bequeath
In a clump of dust. But if they looked beneath:
Here I am,

Still in my cave, complexion like a baby's,
Pink and soft and wonderfully at ease,
Never expelled from the warmth of Mama's womb.

A Lesson in Observation

A Lesson in Observation

Pay close attention: the world that appears now
at zero-point-zero-one degrees
was, as far as is known,
the only one
that burst out of the silence.

It hovered within a blue bubble, fairly large;
and sometimes there were clouds, sea breezes,
sometimes a house, perhaps a kite, children,
and here and there an angel,
or a garden, or a town.
Beneath these were the dead, beneath them
rock, beneath this the fiery prison.

Is that clear? I will repeat: outside there were
clouds, screams, air-to-air missiles,
fire in the fields, memory.
Far beneath these, there were houses, children. What else.

The little dot on the side? It seems to be
the only moon of that world.
It was silent even before this.

Spaceship

Soon I will have to begin. All around me
moons have lit up. Have burned.
I am receiving a different light, perhaps from inside,
like a dim street-lamp
in a city park I once heard of.
And I try to imagine: a city. How was a city possible,
for example? What were the prerequisites
for a tree? For the growth of a bench? For a child?

Now to take off.
There is no time left.
I am preparing myself
to hover over the face of the non-abyss
into my body and onwards

Cursing of the Moon

Assyria

Moon after moon, standing here
at the top of the white tower,
we have longed, O White One,
for thy body,
growing golden, holy and adorned
and elusive.
When the jubilees passed and the reckonings
of the end of days,
and almost we were resigned,
behold, on this night, suddenly
thou didst not refuse:
and we are upon thee, within thee, woe unto us, thou
stricken with the pox of dust, chalked, scarred,
for months – moon after moon – not even dead.

Perhaps we shall remember thee the grace
of our youth.

End of the Questionnaire

Housing conditions: number of galaxy and star,
number of grave.
Are you alone or not.
What grass grows on top of you,
and from where (e.g. from your stomach, eyes, mouth, etc.)

You have the right to appeal.

In the blank space below indicate
how long you have been awake and why are you surprised.

Testimony

Europe, Late

Violins float in the sky,
and a straw hat. I beg your pardon,
what year is it?
Thirty-nine and a half, still awfully early,
you can turn off the radio.
I would like to introduce you to:
the sea breeze, the life of the party,
terribly mischievous,
whirling in a bell-skirt, slapping down
the worried newspapers: tango! tango!
And the park hums to itself:
    I kiss your dainty hand, madame,
    your hand as soft and elegant
    as a white suede glove. You'll see, madame,
    that everything will be all right,
    just heavenly – you wait and see.
    No it could never happen here,
    don't worry so – you'll see – it could

Written in Pencil in the Sealed Railway-Car

here in this carload
i am eve
with abel my son
if you see my other son
cain son of man
tell him i

The Roll Call

He stands, stamps a little in his boots,
rubs his hands. He's cold in the morning breeze:
a diligent angel, who has worked hard for his promotions.
Suddenly he thinks he's made a mistake: all eyes,
he counts again in the open notebook
all the bodies waiting for him in the square,
camp within camp: only I
am not there, am not there, am a mistake,
turn off my eyes, quickly, erase my shadow.
I shall not want. The sum will be in order
without me: here for eternity.

Testimony

No no: they definitely were
human beings: uniforms, boots.
How to explain? They were created
in the image.

I was a shade.
A different creator made me.

And he in his mercy left nothing of me that would die.
And I fled to him, rose weightless, blue,
forgiving – I would even say: apologizing –
smoke to omnipotent smoke
without image or likeness.

Instructions for Crossing the Border

Imaginary man, go. Here is your passport.
You are not allowed to remember.
You have to match the description:
your eyes are already blue.
Don't escape with the sparks
inside the smokestack:
you are a man, you sit in the train.
Sit comfortably.
You've got a decent coat now,
a repaired body, a new name
ready in your throat.
Go. You are not allowed to forget.

Draft of a Reparations Agreement

All right, gentlemen who cry blue murder as always,
nagging miracle makers,
quiet!
Everything will be returned to its place,
paragraph after paragraph.
The scream back into the throat.
The gold teeth back to the gums.
The smoke back to the tin chimney and further on and inside
back to the hollow of the bones,
and already you will be covered with skin and sinews and you
    will live,
look, you will have your lives back,
sit in the living room, read the evening paper.
Here you are. Nothing is too late.
As to the yellow star: immediately
it will be torn from your chest
and will emigrate
to the sky.

Footprints

Footprints

'From heaven to the heaven of heavens to the heaven of night.'
YANNAI

Against my will
I was continued by this cloud: restless, gray,
trying to forget in the horizon, which always recedes

Hail falling hard,
like the chatter of teeth:
refugee pellets pushing eagerly
into their own destruction

In another sector
clouds not yet identified.
Searchlights that set up
giant crosses of light
for the victim.
Unloading of cattle-cars.

Afterwards the letters fly up,
after the flying letters mud
hurries, snuffs, covers for a time

It's true, I was a mistake, I was forgotten
in the sealed car, my body tied up
in the sack of life

Here's the pocket where I found bread,
the sweet crumbs, all of them from the same world

Maybe there's a window here – if you don't mind,
look near that body, maybe you can open up
a bit. That reminds me
(pardon me) of the joke about the two Jews
in the train, they were travelling to

Say something else, talk.
Can I pass from my body and onwards –

*

From heaven to the heaven of heavens to the heaven of night
long convoys of smoke

The new seraphim who haven't yet understood,
prisoners of hope, wandering in the empty freedom,
suspicious as always: how to exploit
this sudden vacuum, maybe
the double citizenship will help,
the old passport,
maybe the cloud? what's new in the cloud,
here too of course
they take bribes. And between us: the biggest bills
are still nicely hidden away, sewn
between the soles –
but the shoes have been piled up below:
a great gaping heap

Convoys of smoke. Sometimes
someone breaks away,
recognizes me for some reason, calls my name.
And I put on a pleasant face, try to remember;
who else
who

Without any right to remember, I remember
a man screaming in a corner, bayonets rising
to fulfill their role
in him

Without any right to remember. What else
was there? Already I'm not afraid
that I might say

without any connection at all:
there was a heart, blue from excessive winter,
and a lamp, round, blue, kind-hearted.
But the kerosene disappears with the blood, the flame
    flickers –

Yes, before I forget:
the rain stole across some border, so did I,
on forbidden escape-routes, with forbidden hope,
we passed the mouth of the pits

Maybe now
I'm looking in that rain
for the scarlet thread

Where to begin?
I don't even know how to ask.
Too many tongues are mixed in my mouth. But
at the crossing of these winds,
very diligent, I immerse myself
in the laws of heavenly grammar: I am learning
the declensions and ascensions of
silence.

> Who has given you the right to jest?
> What is above you you already know.
> You meant to ask about what is within you,
> what is abysmally through you.
> How is it you did not see?

But I didn't know I am alive.
From the heaven of heavens to the heaven of night
angels rushed, sometimes one of them
would look back, see me, shrug his shoulders,
continue from my body and onwards

*

Frozen and burst, clotted,
scarred,
charred, choked.

If it has been ordained that I must pull out of here,
I'll try to descend rung by rung,
I hold on to each one, carefully –
but there is no end to the ladder, and already
no time. All I can still do is fall
into the world

And on my way back
my eyes hint to me:
you have been, what else did you want to see?
Close us and see:
you are the darkness, you are the sign.

And my throat says to me:
if you are still alive, give me an opening, I
must praise.

And my upside-down head is faithful to me,
and my hands hold me tight:
I am falling falling
from heaven to the heaven of heavens to the heaven of night

*

So – a world.
The gray is softened by the blue.
In the gate of this cloud there is already a sweet turquoise
(perhaps light green) innocence. Already sleep.
Heavens renew themselves, try out their wings, see me
and run for their lives. I no longer wonder.

The gate bursts open:
a lake
void void pure of reflections

Over there,
in that arched blue, on the edge of the air,
I once lived. My window was fragile.
Maybe what remained of me
were little gliders that hadn't grown up:
they still repeat themselves in still-clouds, glide,
slice the moment
                    (not to remember now, not to remember)

And before I arrive
                    (now to stretch out to the end, to stretch out)
already awake, spread to the tips of my wings,
against my will guessing that it's very near,
inside, imprisoned by hopes, there flickers
this ball of the earth,
scarred, covered with footprints.

Camouflage

Like

Perhaps she is like the nest of a violin
and bursts
and suddenly flies.

Perhaps she blossoms sweetly in oleander,
like stolen honey on the long tongue
of night-moths.

But ten hearts in the tips of my fingers
are beating: no,
she isn't like

Snake

The sand is swift, overflowing,
burrows inside itself, searching
for remnants, tombstones, ancestors'
bones.
I never understood this hunger
for the past. I
am a series of instants,
shed my skin with ease,
forget,
outsmart myself.
In all this desert only I can guess
who was who.

A Modest Sum

Our forefathers the tortoise and the sea-lizard tramped
Ponderously through the tepid comfort of the swamp.
Their merit did not save us. The jungle climbed,
Spread, burst, and was swept away, a sign of the times.
My teacher, the gorilla, is severe; does not approve
That I'm a modest youngster, considerate, well-behaved.
Every time I'm terrified by the blood or pain,
He shouts: what's wrong with you, when will you be a man!
He's right: I should develop, shouldn't ponder
So much. Should be a well-adjusted hunter.

Twelve Faces of the Emerald

1

I am exceedingly green: chillgreen.
What have I to do
with all the greenishness of chance?
I am the green-source,
the green-self,
one and incomparable.

2

The most suspicious flash
in the cat's eye
at the most acute moment
aspires
to be
me.

3

What have I to do with you, or the living grass?
Among you I am a stranger –
brilliant, cold, playing with my eternities.

4

The emperor Nero, artist in stage-lighting,
raises me to his red eye:
only my green can pacify his blood.
Through me he observes the end of the burning world.

5

Slander! I am not
envious of the diamond: fickle duke,
reckless, lacking in self-control:
daggers! fireworks!
I, on the contrary, am moderate,

know how to bide my time,
to pour, green and accurate,
the poison.

6

As if I shared a secret. Shade of blue,
hint of red in a polished facet,
hesitating violet –
they're gone, they're gone.
I, the green-source,
abolish the colors of the rainbow.

7

You think that you will find your image
in mine.
No. I shall not leave a trace of you;
you never were in me.
Mirror facing mirror facing mirror, enchanted,
I am reflected in I.

8

With one flick of the hand
I smash your days into twelve
green nights.

9

I am all eye.
I shall never sleep.

10

And so I put on a face,
twelve facets apparently transparent.

11

Fragments of light:
they indeed are my soul: I shall not fear.

I shall not die.
I have no need to compromise.

12
You will never find the secret of my power.
I am I: crystallized carbon
with a very small quantity
of chromium oxide.

Encounters

Encounters

You encounter a mirror and look away too late.
What's new, you haven't changed at all. Good-bye, so long.

You meet, almost in secret, a bundle of old papers.
You survived, so did they. What else can you say?

You wander about in veins, in arteries, to the heart-beat, then
to a different beat. This blood too is gone.

And suddenly, in the closet, the photograph: you,
the protruding face-bones, the astonished look,

yes, the same bones. Now you understand:
you didn't even die. You renounced in vain.

And what answer will you return with? since there is no
    question.
You're ready for the encounter, rise and break open the door

and climb down the cellar stairs and introduce yourself to the
    wall

Fragments of an Elegy

I've closed your eyes.
I've returned your hands to their place.
The soles of your feet look at me with pity:
I am superfluous.
I find my hands.
What shall I do with my hands?
I tie my tied shoelaces,
button my buttoned coat.

The new cemetery is spacious,
entirely future. Far, near, incessantly,
the cantors are singing.

You are quiet, a little embarrassed:
perhaps the separation will be long.
The nails are growing, slowly, sketching a truce.
The mouth cavity is at peace with its maker.

But now the earth-fists
are knocking on the boards of the trap:
let us in,
let us in.

Twenty Years in the Valley

And afterwards? I don't know.
Each of us fell
into his own oblivion.

The road got wider and wider. My truck stayed
on the edge, upside-down.
At noon I sometimes look through
its burnt eyes: I don't remember
these cypress trees.
New travellers pass before us, to forget
a different war,
different dead,
faster than us.

But sometimes a wind descends to us,
rustles the wreath
that happened to roll down into the valley,
plucks one petal, then another,
tries to guess:
They love. They love not.
They love
a little. No.
A lot.
No.
Too much.

1968

The Deceased Writer: Photograph in the Rain

And so, Ernie, your laughing head floats along
among black arches, in the cathedral
of an open umbrella.
I read in your wrinkles and am afraid:
storyteller, how did you guess me
before I was.

Your moustache snickers. Already it has reconciled extremes.
You're a monk who has run away in a shabby coat
from the common sense – straight, square – of Manhattan.
You're a heretic, Ernie.
The rain is praying for your nine lives.

This finger of yours is the only thing you never doubted:
it grew up with you, typed your books.
At the end it pulled the trigger
and beckoned to you: come. Everything as foreseen.

Moments of Old Age

1

Someone asks him what day it is. What day?
He doesn't know, he's sorry, he doesn't know why.
The years, the people. Perhaps a different name.
He'll remember it, perhaps, in time.
Sometimes he finds himself in the street, a stranger,
His fingers tightening around the evening paper.
Or suddenly he's in the market, lost in the crush
Of heavy bodies – blue-lipped, gaping like a fish.
In the end, he'll be acquitted and go free –
An old fool who was always asking Why.

2

Stay at home: the future will not move.
A teapot waits and whistles on the stove.
The armchairs have grown thin; the faded rug
Can't understand; a stool like a dog
Lies by your slippered feet. At times a fly
From the world behind your windowpane drops by,
To fly around your head, to try the cake
You courteously offer it, to talk
About its troubles. You listen to it buzz.
No, no, you don't complain that there is no peace.

The Portrait

The little boy
is not sitting still,
it's hard for me to catch the line
of his profile.
I draw one line
and his wrinkles multiply,
dip my brush
and his lips curl, his hair whitens,
his skin, turned blue, peels from his bones. He is not.
The old man is not. And I,
whither shall I go?

From When

Who betrayed me, my heart beat and raged
until it hollowed out a window
from before my silences:
my body sprouts
lilac, my hands
my hands, a bird shrieks
from my mouth.
If only I knew
from when this morning is –
this rushing blood: from when.

Previous Lives

The Tower

I did not want to grow, but quick-fingered memories
which put layer upon layer, each one alone,
were mixed in the tumult of strange tongues,
and left in me unguarded entrances,
stairs that led nowhere,
perspectives that were broken.
Finally, I was abandoned.
Only sometimes in the twisted corridor
a small speechless whisper
still rises in me and runs
like a draught and it seems to me
that I am a whirlwind
whose head is for a moment in the sky
and before I wake up
the mass of my burnt bricks
crumbles
and turns back to clay.

Pages in an Album

Destined to great things, he lies on his belly and confidently
sucks. The expanses of the floor await him:
everything is a target, he can't miss. And already
he's grown up, standing on his feet and forgetting
what he will never learn.
For a moment he enters a class picture and smiles
on the top row, next to the teacher. Meanwhile
with a woman or two, on the beach, footprints
vanishing in the sand. At this time he already rests,
adult and slightly yellowing, in a serious pose,
hand upon forehead, twilight. Even before he has found a
    solution,
he goes on cautiously in the dim corridor, like a thief,
and at the end finds
himself, waiting for himself in the mirror:
the too bright light
of a flashbulb catches
his image
and burns out
the glass lenses of his eyes.

The Seashell

Turned into myself, I was not a seashell for your voice.
I will remain on the unsteady sand.
If a passer-by happened to pick me up,
to try me as an ear, to listen in me for good news
of the sea – I didn't say a word.
With murmuring, with delusive silence,
I gave him back the wide-awake beat
of his blood. As if I had sung: as if he had heard.
Emptier than ever, imprisoned in my convolutions,
how will I live by the commands that you didn't give me,
and on what shore, to what rest's end?
I will remain on the unsteady sand.
I have no escape from your silence.

Come

Come out of your astrology, the order
of constellations imprisoned in wheels
which did not shine for you.
The sign of the scales is balanced.
You are tired. Your vision rising
to distances which you do not find
returns empty into your eyes.
Come: and be gathered into the midst of the darkness
between the lights:
and revolve, extinguished, inside the wheel of your blood.

The Shot

Upside down, he still
waits, and in his ears there is still
just the beginning of a sound,
like the one syllable
of death, an echo
rebounding inside his skull.
A dry drizzle escapes
from the sandbags. A wind
waves the hair and surrenders.
But still he can command
his body's troops, he gives the signal
and the revolution of his eyeballs turns
inward, now he can see:
well then,
a time to keep silence.
He will marshal himself again,
hide in the grass,
lie in ambush
for the things to come.
But his refugee blood
which wandered about in his veins
cannot be imprisoned,
leaves too soon
and cries out from the ground,
the ground which did not open its mouth
and did not want to be his.

The Beginning

In the ice-filled chaos before the end of creation,
distant fleets of steel are waiting.
Boundaries, in secret, mark themselves.
High above the smoke and the odour of fat and skins hovers
a yellow magnetic stain.
Oblique rays at the pole, alert, quick-eyed,
search for the signal. The code is cracked.
Now that all is prepared for darkness,
a wind, with savage fur, from the horizon, blows
in the hollow bones of mountains,
and at the zero-hour
the Great Bear, blazing, strides forth
in heat. The heavens stand now,
and the earth, and all their hosts.
A time of war.

The Cycle

Go to the ant, you sluggard, and go
in the black column between mountain-high furrows
in the way of all your kind
and store the harvest of a grain. Thus
to dust you will return in a crumbling season,
to the deep cells of larvae
to the blind milk-white mass
wriggling with desire
to swarm, to run
in the black column between mountain-high furrows
and in an autumn wind
to store the harvest of a grain which will come
and the straw that is your body.
Consider your ways.

Harvests

The prudent field-mouse
hoards and hoards for the time of battle and siege.
His home is furnished with cunning
passageways; his granary is full.
Above him,
as always, the fire revels in the wheat
and in the heart of the sun, waiting for him –
sharp-eyed, punctual – the hawk.

Ready for Parting

Ready for parting, as if my back were turned,
I see my dead come toward me, transparent and breathing.
I do not accept:
one walk around the square, one rain,
and I am another, with imperfect rims, like clouds.
Grey in the passing town, passing and glad,
among transitory streetlamps,
wearing my strangeness like a coat, I am free to stand
with the people who stand at the opening of a moment
in a chance doorway, anonymous as raindrops
and, being strangers, near and flowing one into another.

Ready for parting, waiting a while in the archway
for the signs of my life which appear in the chipped plaster
and look out from the grimy windowpane. A surprise of
    roses.
Bursting out and already future, twisted into its veins –
a blossoming to every wind. Perhaps
not in my own time into myself and from myself and
    onward
from gate within gate I will go out into the jungle of rain,
free to pass on like one who has tried his strength
I will go out
from the space in between as if from the walls of denial.

Scarabs

At noon you go back to the dust
of cities plowed and harvested and uncover potsherds
from the sockets of their eyes. Now, in what century,
according to what broken calendar, passes before you
the rider who crumbled in the wind,
and returns to the harvest of arrows and swords, like you.
Astonished in the wind of ashes,
he bends the empty bow of his eyebrows, searches
for treasures of gold and straw.

All is left undecided. And begins forever
in the dust where – black, speechless –
scarabs,
with all their feet,
knead bricks for the walls and storehouses
of treasure cities,
and the blood splashes in the clay.

Already

Already I was before I am
forced in a surprised night wind to return
exhausted in dry grass and obeying
the command of a nagging voice.
On the main road bright candles for the dead
told me to come:
the house, the strange name lying in wait for me
in these veins of darkness. Closed
between my blood and my blood, in the blind warmth
folded inside me, kicking from within me to leave
the sweet hollow and to suddenly cry out
in the air running through the lungs.
Already I am not
(I was a distant summer) and at this moment,
when I must see the other light, I am
that I am. Already
I do not remember.

Final Examination

'If I am not mistaken:
the lightning that disappeared
only now pierces
the eye.
The air that has taken the place
of the severed hand
only now hurts
the cripple.'

– No, that is not right. Memory is not there.
What you said is only a parable.
But you, my servant, you
must be precise. I expected more from you.
It doesn't matter. Do not fear, my servant. You will not fail.
Think. Think again, well, and answer me:
Where is memory?
Who has pierced?
What was severed?

Brain

Brain

1

In the dark night of the skull
he suddenly discovers
he's born.

A difficult moment.

Since then he's been very busy.
He thinks
that he thinks that
and he goes around and around:
where's the way out?

If, in some world, there were things,
he of course would love them very much,
he would give names to them all.
For instance: Brain.
That's me. Brain. I'm it.

Ever since his exile, he reasons:
there must have been a place to rest.

2

How will he move the darkness?

Brain hovers upon the face of the deep.
But now two deep wounds burst
in the bones of the forehead. Eyes.
The eyes betray to him
the world: here, spread out before him,
a world, complete, solid:

look, Brain is hovering
just five feet four inches above the floor!
Now that the truth is out
he is overwhelmed by vertigo:
five feet four!
Alone upon the face of the deep.

3
He has a suspicion
that in the whole universe of the skull
there is no other brain but him.

Then, a new suspicion:
that myriads of brains are imprisoned in him,
packed together,
splitting off from him, betraying him from within,
surrounding him.

And he doesn't know which evil
is the lesser.

4
True, he's not handsome, but
he's interesting-looking:
greyish-white convolutions,
a bit oily, sliding back and forth.
Silver curls inside the skull?
Oh no, Brain resembles
nothing else in the world,
except perhaps
the small intestine.

5
This is a mountain.
This is a woman.
But immediately Brain deciphers:

Not a mountain. An upside-down valley.
Not a woman. A body putting up a front.
Only the cave fever
gripping the blood
is still the same desire.

6

Brain makes a friend, a shut-in like himself.
They both have radio sets
and in their spare time
they broadcast to each other from the attic.
Brain asks for example:
Have you got syllogisms? Alarm centres?
Six hundred million memory cells?
And how do you feel inside your cranium, Brain?

Sometimes he jokes around:
Have you heard any good ones lately?
Have you seen any good ones, Brain,
have you smelled any, tasted any?
(And all along he knows his sixth sense
is the most sensational of the five.)
But his friend is upset:
You're getting on my nerves, Brain.

After a while he becomes really intimate with him
and broadcasts some strictly personal problems:
Tell me, do you know how to forget?

7

One of his fears: that he still has hieroglyphs
carved inside him.
He is the twisted brain
of Pharaoh on his deathbed.
Pharaoh is not yet ready.
Before they mummify him

they pierce both his nostrils
and suck out
the cold contents of his skull.

8
Brain number three hundred and twenty five? Here.
Number seven? Here.
Number six hundred thousand nine hundred and seven?
   Here.
Number zero? Here.
Number one? Number one! Where is brain number one?

9
Mid-way into my death, in bitter grief
About my life's mid-way, being still ensnared
In a bush of veins, dark, with no relief,

In a bush of veins, still waiting for the word,
There suddenly burst out before I knew
This blood of mine, my servant and my lord –

Why did I speak. Whom did I speak to. No,
It wasn't this I wanted to announce.
Hello? Who's there, who's listening? Hello?

10
The internal veins of the head extend to the brain's
anterior base; from these radiate the veins of the
proencephalon, the mesencephalon, and the metenceph-
alon. The brain shell, although it is very thin (very),
contains the great majority of the neurons in the nervous
system (in man approximately 10 billion). The brain is
the organ of time. A dog from which the cerebrum has
been removed is still able to live for a time, but only
in the present. All the doggish past vanishes instantly,
and the doggish future already does not exist.

Brain yawns: he is embarrassed by so much praise.
Those marvelous symbols: Who invented them?
Brain. And the paper? Brain.
And me?
But Brain has learned to defend himself
from such attacks.
He gives a sign: Let there be darkness!
And at once
the fingers shut the encyclopedia.

11

He would like to be faithful
only to himself,
to be pure and void,
void of memory like a mirror.

12

He is a moon whose two sides
are forever dark.

13

Brain counts
seconds on his journey from one star to the next.
Years on his journey from one grain of sand to the next.
Aeons on his longest journey: to Brain.

14

A time of peace. He pampers himself a bit
by thinking
that far away, somewhere in outer space,
in some unguessed-at nebula,
between the stars that melt to milky haze,
some Purpose is waiting for him – still obscure,
but his, entirely his. Tomorrow, or
the day after tomorrow (who can tell?)
he may strip off his sombre prison clothes,
and in a nut-shell

blithely he'll take off, and fly, and land,
the sovereign of worlds without end.

15
Brain gropes around: he is surrounded.
No refuge in the skull.
Inside the maze twists
the maze.

Brain is now enormous: a grey cloud,
a very heavy cloud. In the throat of this cloud
sticks
a jagged lightning-bolt.

Wait a second: Brain hears himself
ticking off the seconds.
A time-bomb?
He wasn't ready for that.
He was off his guard.

But Brain shakes himself free
and declares: I'm just a dream.

16
Brain receives signals
through immense distances.
From space, from a depth dark-years away,
a living code reaches him,
another world broadcasting ceaselessly, like himself,
sleeplessly, like himself,
knowledgelessly.

A heart?

17
Brain, pleased, surveys his centers:
a center for speech, a center for lies.

a center for memory
(seventy clocks, at least, each keeping its own time),
a special center for pain –
Suddenly he hears the astounding news:
There is a hidden circle somewhere
whose center is everywhere
and whose circumference is nowhere:
a center which is so near
that he will never
be able
to see it.

18
Now he sees what is to come:
he will depart slowly, reluctantly,
and in some disorder.
First
his fear deserts him.

Then he is without the sarcasm,
the joking around,
the puns.
Then his conjectures are disconnected.
He lingers on for a while: something was here once,
very near, a nuisance. What could it have been –

Then he no longer has to remember.

Then
he is quite forgotten,

and he is light.

More about Penguins and Pelicans

Penguinews, which appears every month, contains details of all the new books issued by Penguins as they are published. From time to time it is supplemented by *Penguins in Print*, which is our complete list of almost 5,000 titles.

A specimen copy of *Penguinews* will be sent to you free on request. Please write to Dept EP, Penguin Books Ltd, Harmondsworth, Middlesex, for your copy.

In the U.S.A.: For a complete list of books available from Penguins in the United States write to Dept CS, Penguin Books Inc., 7110 Ambassador Road, Baltimore, Maryland 21207.

In Canada: For a complete list of books available from Penguins in Canada write to Penguin Books Canada Ltd, 41 Steelcase Road West, Markham, Ontario.